CONTENTS

INTRODUCTION

The current Queensland handwriting script was introduced in 1985. Its print style, the Beginner's Alphabet, is based on simple, italic cursive shapes that are easily joined to become Queensland Modern Cursive. Because the capitals remain the same, the two scripts merge easily, so children find cursive writing easier to write as well as to read. Queensland Modern Cursive is designed to be fluent and quick, with maximum legibility.

FOCUS

- carefully sequenced and thorough handwriting program
- revision of cursive elements on single letters (joins rocket reference card included)
- progressive revision of cursive joins from two- or three-letter combinations to words
- writing on 4 mm red and blue lines
- high interest thematic passages
- large join examples highlight correct direction and rotation
- integrated activities
- Theme: space.

TECHNIQUE

Pencil grip

1. The thumb and the index finger support the pencil while it rests on the middle finger.
2. Child should be able to tap the pencil with the pointer finger while it is supported by the middle finger and thumb.
3. There should be a distance of approx. 2–2.5 cm from the pencil point to the tip of the index finger, 3 cm for a left-hander. Rubber bands are useful markers. Triangular pencil-grips promote correct finger placement and distance.

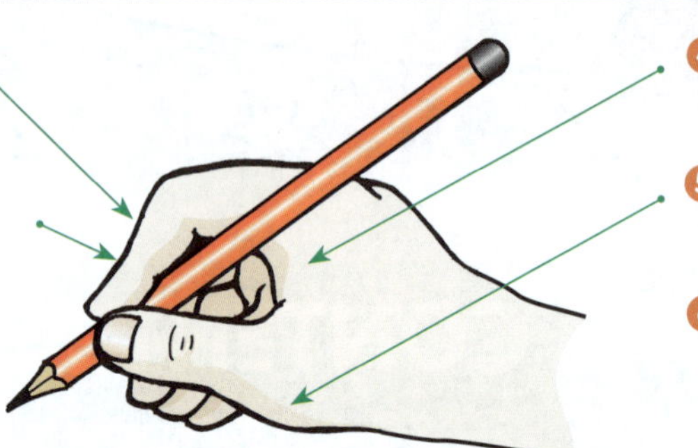

4. Hold pencil barrel up high, near or before the knuckle. Pencil should not rest low in the "web" of the hand.
5. The side of the hand and the little finger act as supports for the whole hand.
6. Unpainted pencils are less slippery.

Posture

Right-handers

1. Keep back straight at an angle of about 30° to back of chair, and keep bottom towards back of seat.

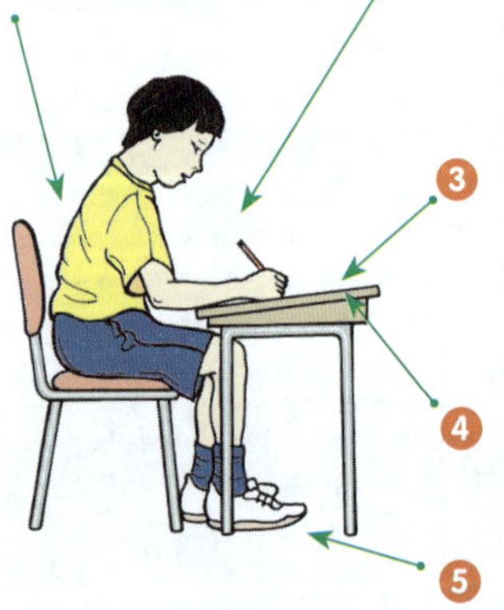

2. Make sure that book or paper is sufficient distance from the edge of the desk to enable most/all of the forearm to rest on the desk. Move book up as child works down the page to maintain this.
3. Table or desk height about level with child's waistline or a bit higher. The weight of the body is supported by the non-writing arm.
4. Sloping desks are ideal, especially for struggling writers.
5. Feet should touch the floor.

Left-handers

Left-handers should have their elbow in to discourage a hooked wrist.

Paper position

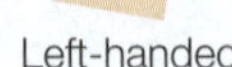

Left-handed

Right-handed

Right-handed

GENERAL TEACHING TIPS

- Display joins rocket (see reference card) and the cursive alphabet across the top of the board.
- Contact joins rocket (see reference card) to children's desks.
- Model handwriting on the blackboard one word at a time to help internalise letter and join shape and direction.
- Encourage slope.
- Soft sharp HB pencils (unpainted) are recommended for upper levels.

Please see further information on the learning features of this book on page 3, and Teacher's Notes on page 63.

LEARNING FEATURES

Clear lesson focus

Large example to trace, including arrows for correct rotation

Thorough practice from two- or three-letter combinations to words

High-frequency spelling or reading words where possible.

High interest space words

Space-theme based non-fiction passages add interest

Space allows teacher to target individual needs

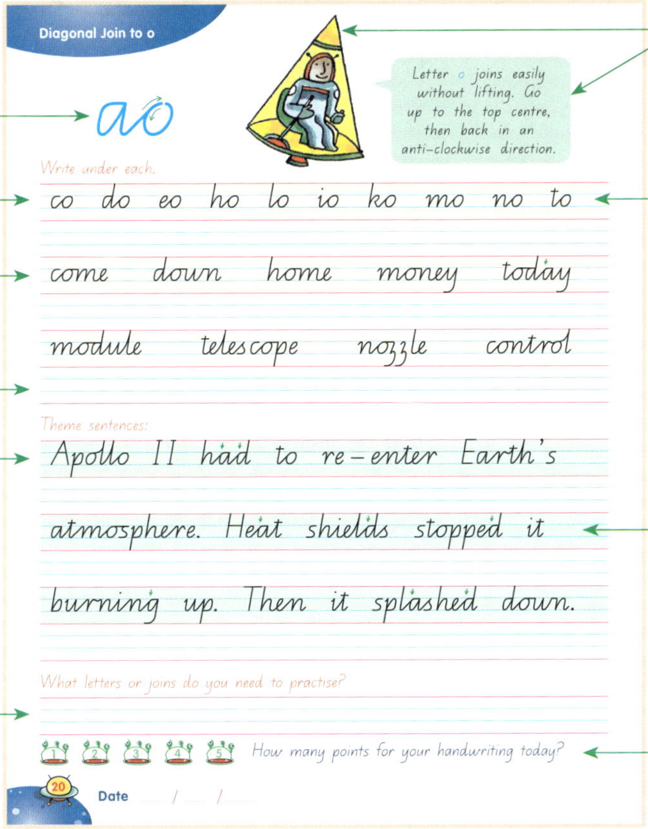

Diagonal Join to o

ao

Letter o joins easily without lifting. Go up to the top centre, then back in an anti-clockwise direction.

Write under each.

co do eo ho lo io ko mo no to

come down home money today

module telescope nozzle control

Theme sentences:

Apollo 11 had to re-enter Earth's atmosphere. Heat shields stopped it burning up. Then it splashed down.

What letters or joins do you need to practise?

1 2 3 4 5 How many points for your handwriting today?

20 Date / /

Attractive thematic illustration with helpful advice. Theme: Space

Only possible letter combinations are given

Carefully sequenced program revising all groups: entries and exits to diagonal joins, horizontal joins, pencil lifts, dropping on, sweep up joins and doubles.

Generous spacing for larger writing

Self-evaluation

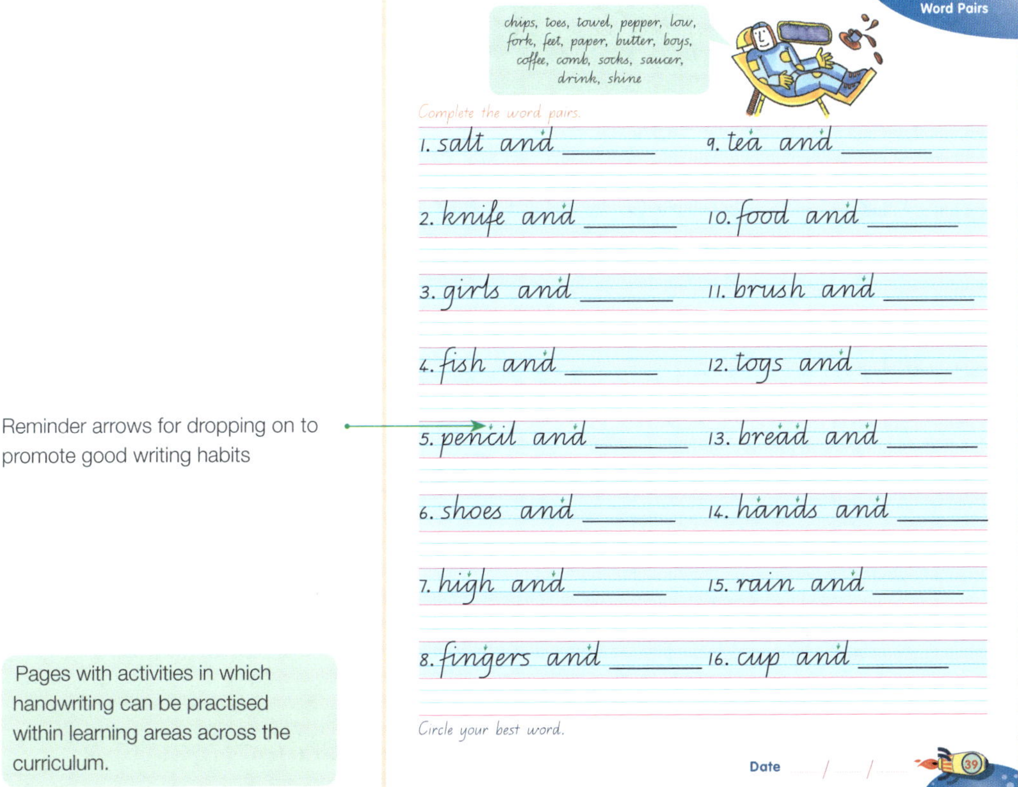

Reminder arrows for dropping on to promote good writing habits

Pages with activities in which handwriting can be practised within learning areas across the curriculum.

Sections are colour-coded for easy reference:

- Yellow: skills development
- Green: sentence
- Blue: activities from across the curriculum

A useful joins train reference card and handwriting certificate provided

Write under each letter, then put it into the correct carriage.

a b c d e f g h i j k l m

n o p q r s t u v w x y z

abcdefghijklmnopqrstuvwxyz

Try these alphabet sentences.

Pack my box with five dozen quality

purple jugs. The quick brown fox

jumped over the lazy guard dogs.

What letters or joins do you need to practise?

1 2 3 4 5 How many points for your handwriting today?

Date ..../........../..........

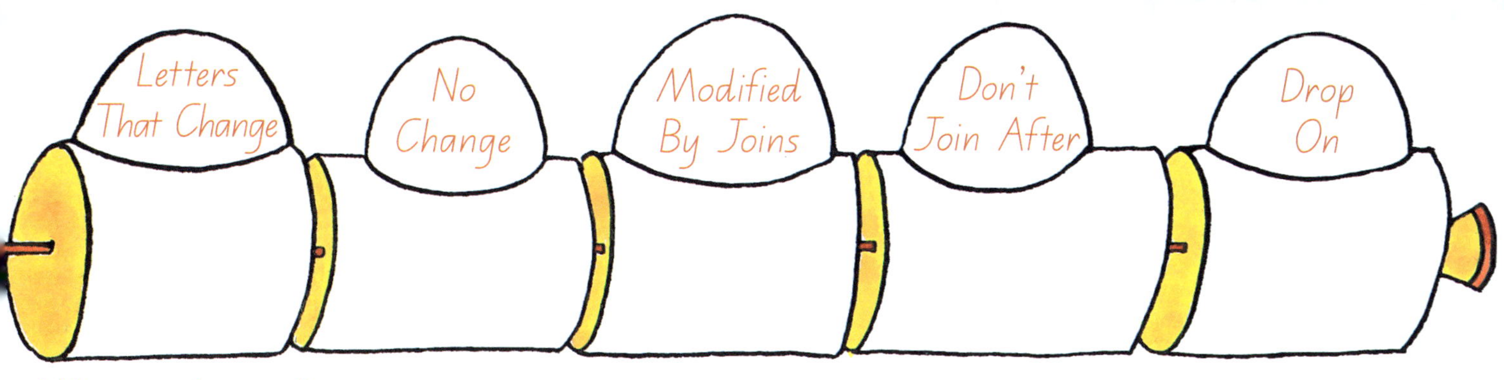

Write under each.

The solar system is the Sun and all

the planets, moons, asteroids and other

objects that revolve, or orbit, around it.

Theme sentences:

Earth is the only planet in our solar

system with abundant water and life.

It spins on its axis and orbits the Sun.

What letters or joins do you need to practise?

Circle your best word.

Date ..../........../..........

ai

Stretch up at a slippery-slide angle for diagonal joins.

Write under each.

ci du ev hi ku ly mu ni ty av

cut lies said why key ever

Jupiter universe supply gravity

Theme sentence:

If animals could survive a rocket launch of 28 000 km per hour and the heat of re-entry, humans could, too.

What letters or joins do you need to practise?

 1  2  3  4  5

How many points for your handwriting today?

Date ..../........../..........

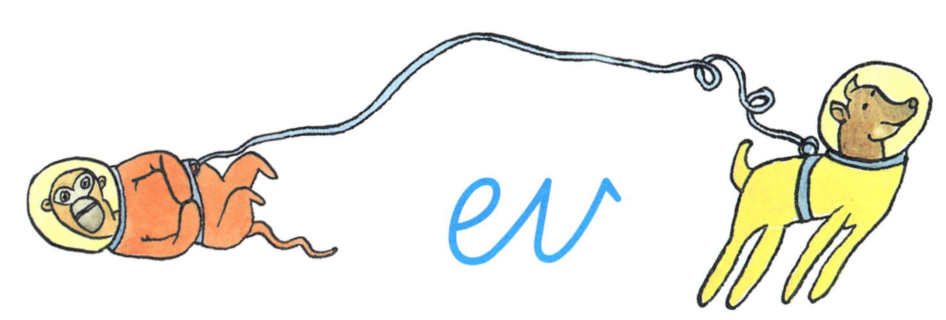

Stretch out to separate letters.

Write under each.

iv ev cu di nu mi hy ti av li

five kite twin they time even

Neptune swivel spacesuit Sputnik

Theme sentence:

More than fifteen cats and dogs,

four monkeys and many mice were

launched between 1948 and 1952.

What letters or joins do you need to practise?

Circle your best word.

Date .... / .... / ....

an

Make sure your rounded entries look different to your pointed entries.

Write under each.

an am ar en em er in im ir

then film girl many them

atmosphere lunar engines crater

Theme sentences:

In 1952, two monkeys, Mike and Patricia, became the first space animals to return alive. In 1960, two dogs did, too.

What letters or joins do you need to practise?

1 2 3 4 5 How many points for your handwriting today?

Date  .... / .... / ....

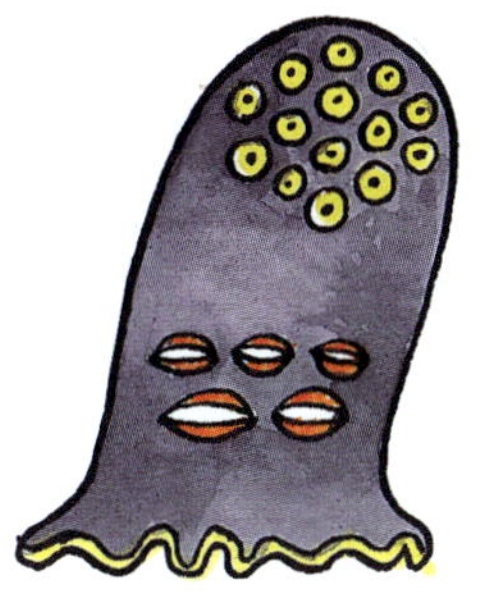

With x, do the exit before you cross it. Drop on the next letter, any letter.

Write under each.

ax ex ix ux ax ex ix ux ax ex

axle next sixty-six except taxi

galaxy oxygen exhaust explore axis

Theme sentences:

1961—Yuri Gagarin became the first

person in space. He orbited the Earth

once in the Soviet spacecraft, Vostok 1.

What letters or joins do you need to practise?

Circle your best word.

Date ..../........../..........

Put a word that makes sense into each space.

Since 1961, every space 1. _____ includes animals and insects so astronauts can observe how they 2. _____. Bees have 3. _____ honeycomb, frogs have laid eggs, fish hatchlings 4. _____ grown and 5. _____ have spun webs. Scientists want to know if 6. _____ radiation and no gravity will 7. _____ them and us.

1 2 3 4 5 How many points for your handwriting today?

Date ..../........../..........

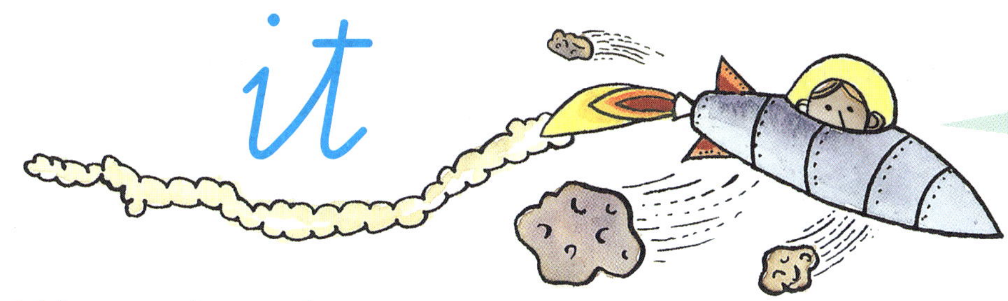

Finish all letters in each word, then go back to dot i and cross t.

Write under each.

in im ir ix it tu ty tw te ti

this sister white eight thing

Jupiter pilot orbit ignite history

Theme sentence:

Astronauts are modern-day explorers

discovering what lies beyond Earth

and learning more about the Universe.

What letters or joins do you need to practise?

Circle your best word.

Date ..../........../..........

ne

Stretch out the exit at the angle of a slippery slide to start letter e.

Write under each.

ae ce de he ie ke le me te ue

home name when date blue

Neptune module telescope engines

Theme sentence:

The first woman to fly in space was

Valentina Tereshkova on Vostok 6 in

1963, orbiting Earth forty-eight times.

What letters or joins do you need to practise?

How many points for your handwriting today?

Date .... / .... / ....

Cross f upwards to join onto the next letter.

Write under each.

fa fe fi fo fu fr fy fl ft

fast fell find four full from

fuel flight fly-by free-fall future

Theme sentence:

1965 — Cosmonaut Alexei Leonov of
the spacecraft Voshod 2 went on the
first spacewalk while tied to it.

What letters or joins do you need to practise?

Circle your best word.

Date ..../........../..........

Take off! Make your own rocket with a balloon, a drinking straw, tape, a clip and some string.

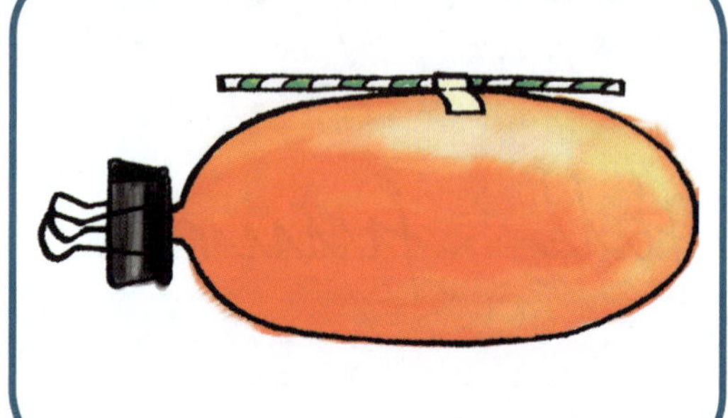

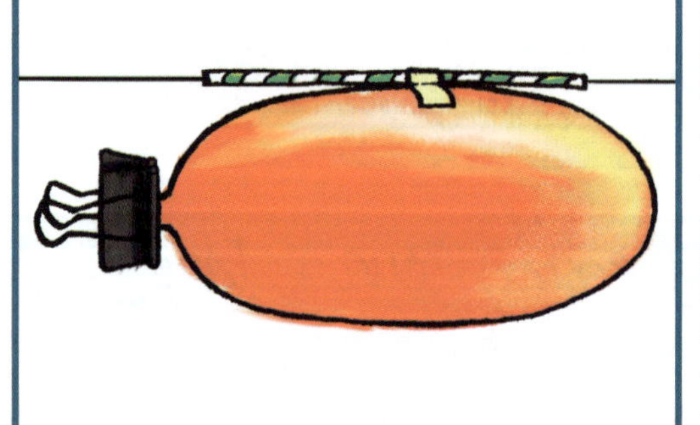

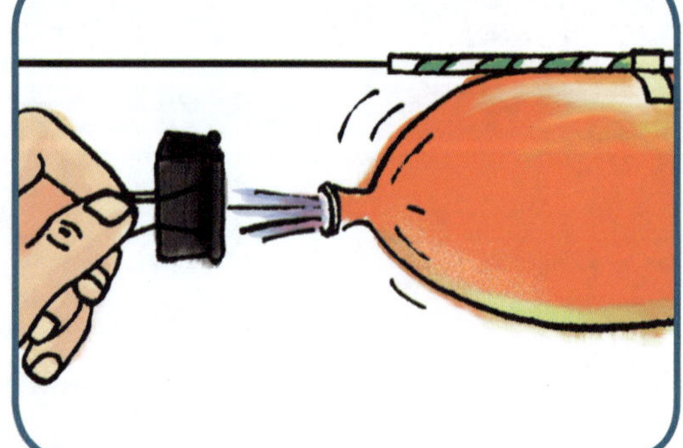

Copy this passage.

Blow up a balloon

and clip it closed.

Attach a straw with

tape. Pass string through

the straw and tie it

tightly between two

chairs. Launch by

releasing the clip.

Date .... / .... / ....

az

Letter z finishes flat on the line, like g, j and y.

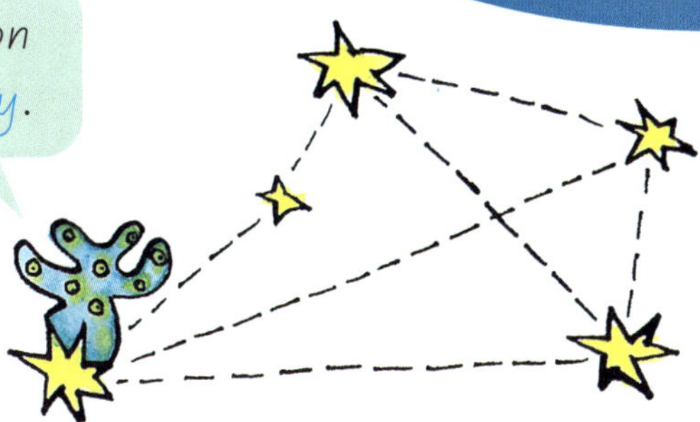

Write under each.

az ez iz uz az ez iz uz az ez

prize amazing hazel breeze lizard

horizon magazine Soyuz Shenzhou

Theme sentences:

A rocket is propelled by a jet of

burning fuel mixed with oxygen.

Fuel tanks fall away to save weight.

What letters or joins do you need to practise?

Circle your best word.

Date ..../........../..........

nmr

Correct entries and open wedges help to tell these letters apart.

Write under each.

an am ar en em er in im ir un

ankle number army under lemon

Saturn astronaut cosmonaut monitor

Theme sentence:

To plan the landing on the Moon,

many space probes were sent to orbit,

photograph, land and travel on it.

What letters or joins do you need to practise?

5 How many points for your handwriting today?

Date .... / .... / ....

u w v

Correct entries and open wedges help to tell these letters apart.

Write under each.

au av aw eu ev ew tu iv lu ui

aunt have away blew alive

countdown runway event Surveyor

Theme sentences:

It is 384 460 km to the Moon, which took Apollo 11 about three days to reach. It had three parts or modules.

What letters or joins do you need to practise?

Circle your best word.

Date ..../........../..........

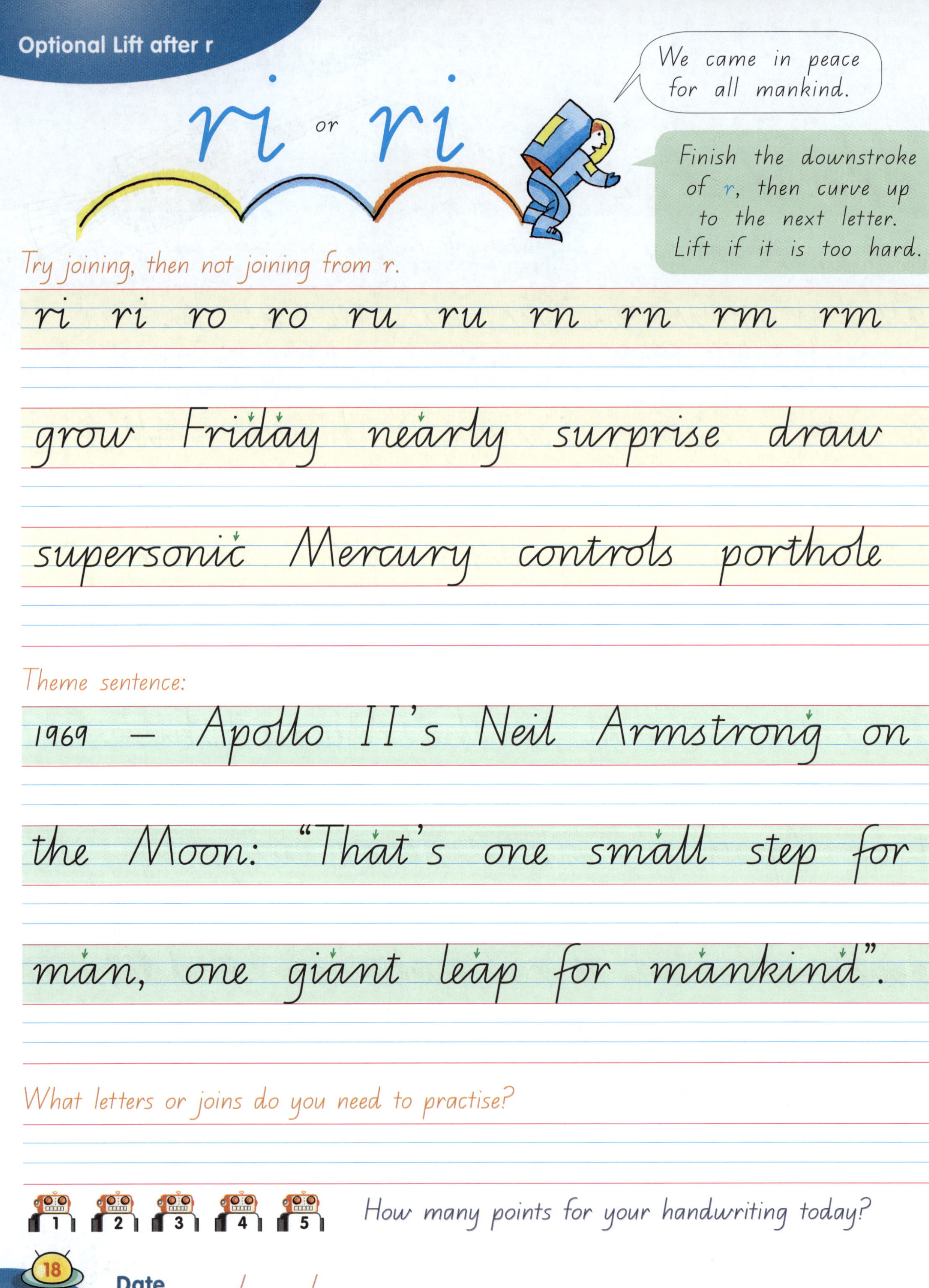

Try joining, then not joining from r.

ri ri ro ro ru ru rn rn rm rm

grow Friday nearly surprise draw

supersonic Mercury controls porthole

Theme sentence:

1969 – Apollo 11's Neil Armstrong on the Moon: "That's one small step for man, one giant leap for mankind".

What letters or joins do you need to practise?

1 2 3 4 5 How many points for your handwriting today?

Date ..../........../..........

Write under each.

square unique aqua quest quickly

squeeze liquid request sequins equip

quarantine Quintuplet – Cluster

Theme sentence:

The crew collected over 21 kg

of rock samples for scientific study

during their 150 minute moonwalk.

What letters or joins do you need to practise?

Circle your best word.

Date ..../........../..........

Letter o joins easily without lifting. Go up to the top centre, then back in an anti-clockwise direction.

Write under each.

co do eo ho lo io ko mo no to

come down home money today

module telescope nozzle control

Theme sentences:

Apollo 11 had to re-enter Earth's atmosphere. Heat shields stopped it burning up. Then it splashed down.

What letters or joins do you need to practise?

1 2 3 4 5 How many points for your handwriting today?

Date .... / .... / ....

Rules: — Chop off e before adding -ing.
— If there is a vowel before a consonant, double the consonant before adding -ing.
— Two vowels, just add -ing.

Write under the words, adding "-ing" as you go.

hatch	dive	shop	begin
close	march	knit	toast
swim	sing	hope	paddle
hop	skip	wipe	squat
cook	wash	joke	flash
cut	let	guide	measure
fly	stop	wriggle	drive
dance	scrub	dream	ski

Circle your best "-ing" word.

Date ..../........../..........

Curve up to the top of tall letters. Don't lift your pencil.

Write under each.

ab ah ak al at eb eh el ck ch

think until children thought help

airlock data thermal backpack

Theme sentence:

Space suits had life-support for four hours—oxygen, heating and cooling, camera, communication, boots, gloves.

What letters or joins do you need to practise?

How many points for your handwriting today?

Date ..../........../..........

If a letter finishes in this direction, it doesn't join to the next letter.

Write under each.

aba aya ebe eye ibi iyi ubu uyu

began your behind year banana

stand-by Voyager Skylab Hubble

Theme sentences:

The first astronauts ate paste from tubes and packets of bite-sized pieces of food. Drinks came with straws.

What letters or joins do you need to practise?

Circle your best word.

Date .... / .... / ....

Write under each.

asa apa ese epe isi ipi usu upu

shout paper should puppy stay

Neptune power space probe payload

Theme sentence:

1981 — The first re-usable space shuttle,

Columbia, lifts off like a rocket, orbits

like a satellite, then glides like a plane.

What letters or joins do you need to practise?

1 2 3 4 5 How many points for your handwriting today?

Date ..../........../..........

Any letter that finishes flat doesn't join.

Write under each.

aja aga aza eje ege eze ugu uzu

just page zero jump pizza girl

magnetic signal Spitzer Sojourner

Theme sentence:

A shuttle has 3 rocket engines and two booster rockets equal to 140 jumbo jets to place it in orbit at 28 175 km/h.

What letters or joins do you need to practise?

Circle your best word.

Date .... / .... / ....

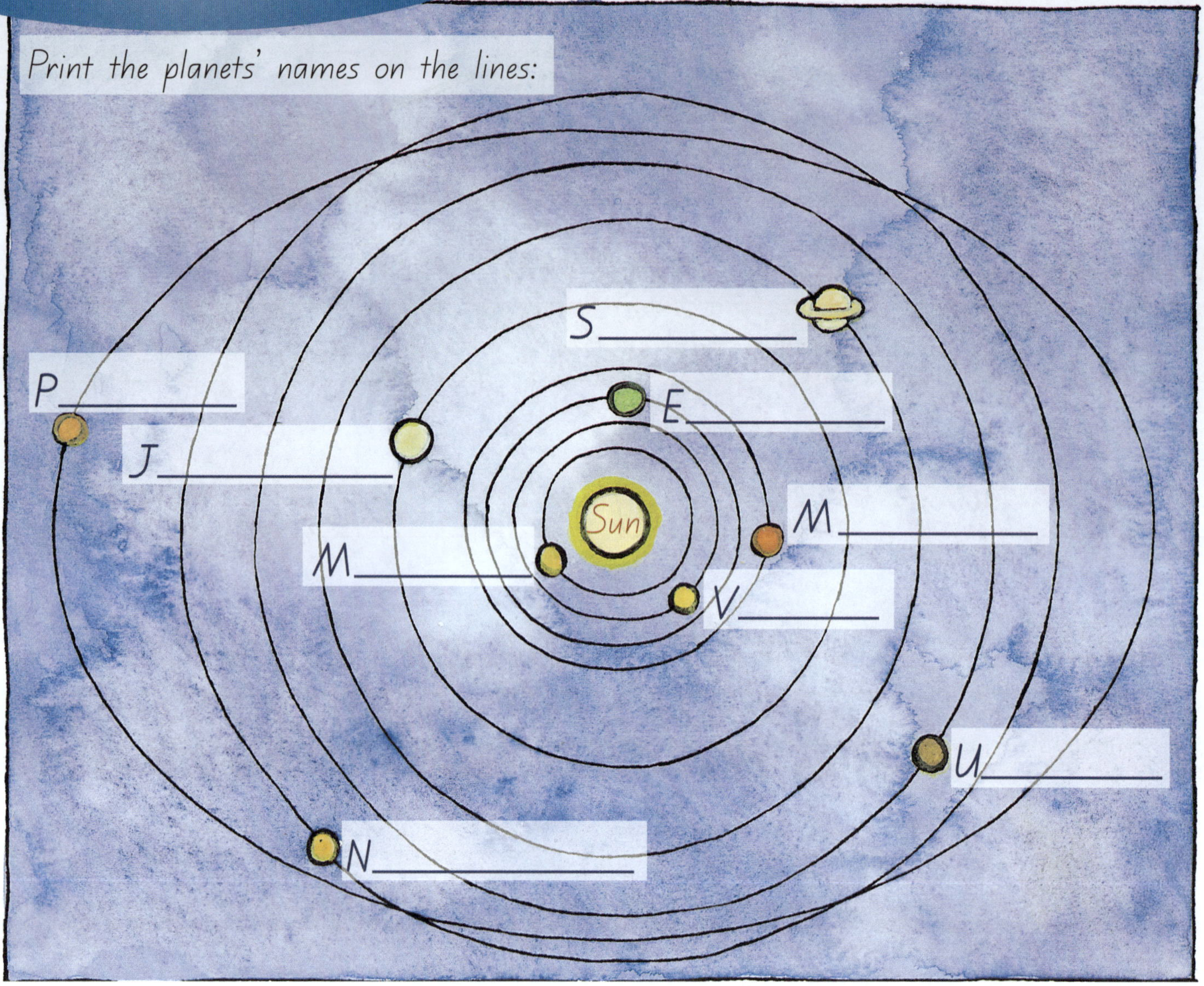
Print the planets' names on the lines:
S
P
E
J
Sun
M
M
V
U
N

The Solar System: Sun, Mercury,

Venus, Earth, Mars, Jupiter,

Saturn, Uranus, Neptune and Pluto.

Date .... / .... / ....

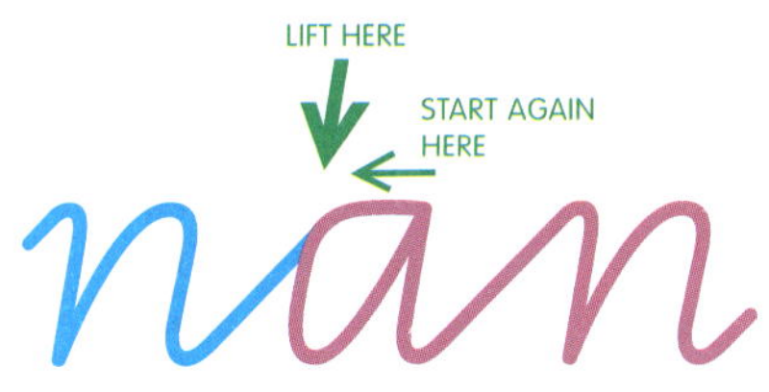

Bring the exit up high to the top blue line, then write the "shoulder", or flat top, to meet it.

Write under each.

l last m make c can't h have

action space start quick black

stand-by lunar solar nuclear

Theme sentences:

1984 — The first untethered spacewalks are made by shuttle astronauts. They used gas, jet-propelled backpacks.

What letters or joins do you need to practise?

Circle your best word.

Date ..../........../..........

a

A high exit at a slippery-slide angle separates the letters before dropping on.

Write under each.

i idea a ago e equal a add i ignore

cold sing equator send eighty

landing radar Chandra X-Ray

Theme sentences:

A satellite is any small object that orbits around a bigger object. The Moon is a natural satellite of Earth.

What letters or joins do you need to practise?

How many points for your handwriting today?

Date .... / .... / ....

Letters that finish near the top go straight across the top blue line to the next letter. Don't lift your pencil.

Write under each.

oa oc og on om op or ov ow oy

boat house show along around

soars odometer meteor asteroid

Theme sentence:

Artificial satellites are human-made and launched into space to orbit Earth and transmit or gather information.

What letters or joins do you need to practise?

Circle your best word.

Date ..../........../..........

vi

The downstroke on v and w now goes straight across the blue line. Don't lift your pencil.

Write under each.

va wa vi wi vu wu vo wo vy wy

win visit won't voice swing

gravity observatory Endeavour

Theme sentences:

A satellite needs enough speed so gravity can't pull it back to Earth. The first was a metal ball with four aerials.

What letters or joins do you need to practise?

How many points for your handwriting today?

Date 

Half a rocket won't get me far!

Draw in the rest of the pieces. Label them.

1. one-half of a sandwich

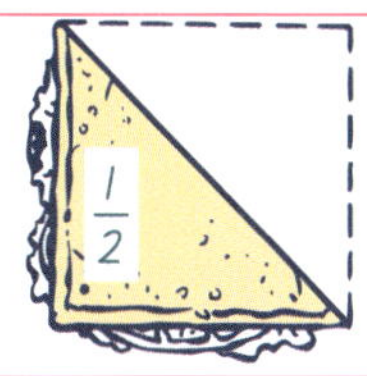

2. one-quarter of a pizza

3. one-third of a lasagne

4. one-sixth of a chocolate

5. one-half of a pancake

6. one-third of a cake

7. one-quarter of a sandwich

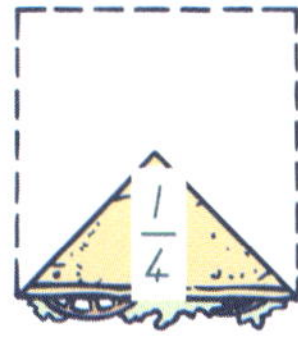

8. one-sixth of a pie

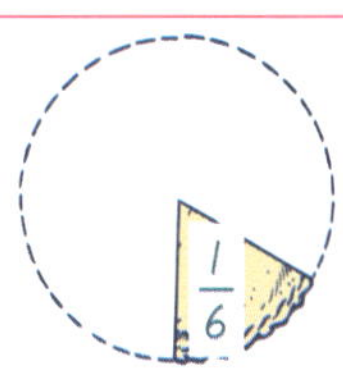

Circle your best word.

Date ..../......../........

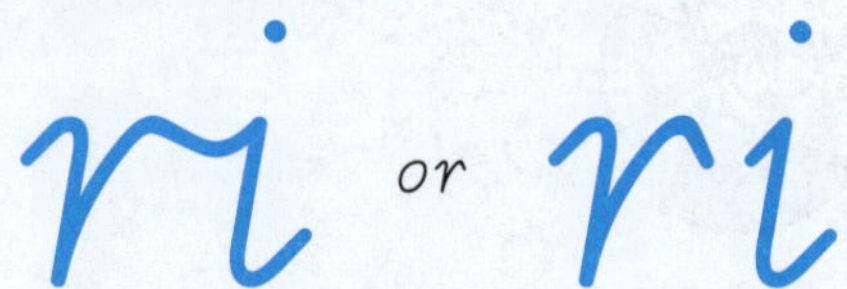

Dip after r to finish it before joining. Lift if it is too hard.

Try joining from r, then lifting after r.

rip rip run run arm arm

dried burn warm learn drive

Saturn thrusters world Discovery

Theme sentence:

Depending on a satellite's purpose,

its orbit around Earth can be

polar, circular or elliptical.

What letters or joins do you need to practise?

How many points for your handwriting today?

Date ..../........../..........

Finish r with a flick, then drop on a, c, d, g, q.

Write under each.

r rack r radar r rail r rapid

yard draw order record train

Mercury Uranus crater Stardust

Theme sentences:

Satellites relay phone calls, T.V. and Internet signals. They navigate ships and cars and track weather and currents.

What letters or joins do you need to practise?

Circle your best word.

Date ..../........../..........

oe

Avoid a droopy join to e— lift after o, r, v, w.

Write under each.

oe re ve we ready twelve

canoe threw alive does before

return atmosphere measure infrared

Theme sentence:

Satellites watch volcanoes, forest fires or logging, track wildlife, locate minerals, measure climate change and spy.

What letters or joins do you need to practise?

How many points for your handwriting today?

Date ..../........../..........

Curve up to the top of the tall letters. Don't lift your pencil.

Write under each.

ob ol ok ot rl rh rk rt wh wl

when party other slowly north

Earth porthole autopilot Vostok

Theme sentences:

1971 — Astronauts can stay for a year doing research and experiments.

Spacecraft deliver food, water, oxygen.

What letters or joins do you need to practise?

Circle your best word.

Date ..../........../..........

Put to, too or two in the spaces.

Write under each.

1. At eight o'clock Toby went ___ bed.

2. May Samantha come to the pool, ___?

3. I'll need ___ dollars for the bus.

4. I'd like an ice-cream ___, please.

5. Matt was so hungry he ate ___ bowls!

6. Let's go ___ the park for a while.

7. It's a long way ___ school from here.

8. ___ birds are building a nest.

Date .... / .... / ....

Add a long join to the front of f only when needed. The shoulder on f causes a loop.

Write under each.

af ef if of uf lf rf wf af ef

often soft loaf gift surf safe

surface infrared refuel artificial

Theme sentences:

1990 — Hubble Space Telescope launched.

It is the size of a bus with

290 square metres of solar panels.

What letters or joins do you need to practise?

Circle your best word.

Date ..../........../..........

fife

Use f without a join at the beginning of a word and after a pencil lift. Add a join to f only when needed.

Write under each.

faf fef fif fof fuf faf fef fif

fire bonfire fast breakfast fry stirfry

fort comfort flow overflow fill refill

Theme sentences:

Hubble's telescope can see infrared

and ultra-violet light. It has taken

thousands of photos of the Universe.

What letters or joins do you need to practise?

1 2 3 4 5

How many points for your handwriting today?

Date ..../........../..........

chips, toes, towel, pepper, low, fork, feet, paper, butter, boys, coffee, comb, socks, saucer, drink, shine

Complete the word pairs.

1. salt and ________
2. knife and ________
3. girls and ________
4. fish and ________
5. pencil and ________
6. shoes and ________
7. high and ________
8. fingers and ________
9. tea and ________
10. food and ________
11. brush and ________
12. togs and ________
13. bread and ________
14. hands and ________
15. rain and ________
16. cup and ________

Circle your best word.

Date ..../........../..........

Cut the shoulder off s after a diagonal join. This is "modified s" or "s with a join".

Join printed s, then modified s.

as as es es is is us us ts ts

east west noise escape asked

Venus spacesuit samples telescope

Theme sentence:

In 1999, the powerful Chandra X-Ray Observatory was launched into Earth's orbit by the space shuttle Columbia.

What letters or joins do you need to practise?

How many points for your handwriting today?

Date .... / .... / ....

Turn S into s

Write under each.

sent present serve preserve

sure measure sick seasick

stone gemstone spoon teaspoon

Theme sentences:

Small, long, thin Orion craft are replacing shuttles. They carry six crew. Cargo is launched separately.

What letters or joins do you need to practise?

Circle your best word.

Date ..../........../..........

S

Use printed s at the beginning of a word.

Write under each.

skip shop school shout seven

scared slide south sugar sudden

supplies splashdown space-walk

Theme sentence:

Orbiter shuttles are equipped with a robot arm for moving satellites into and out of the cargo/payload bay.

What letters or joins do you need to practise?

How many points for your handwriting today?

.... / .... / ....

togs

Write under each.

eggs boys plays pigs always

myself observe upstairs sixty-six

capsule system website top-secret

Theme sentences:

Old space stations and satellites re-enter the atmosphere. Small junk burns up, but larger pieces fall to ocean or land.

What letters or joins do you need to practise?

Circle your best word.

Date .... / .... / ....

Use printed s after a horizontal join. Don't lift your pencil.

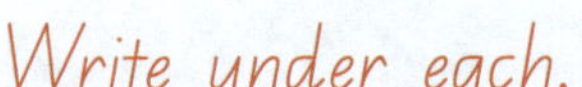

Write under each.

os rs ws os rs ws os rs

post chairs horse knows kilos

Mars light-years Tiros Voskhod

Theme sentences:

Space junk from exploding rockets

orbits Earth and can damage working

satellites. Old spacecraft orbit the Sun.

What letters or joins do you need to practise?

How many points for your handwriting today?

Date .... / .... / ....

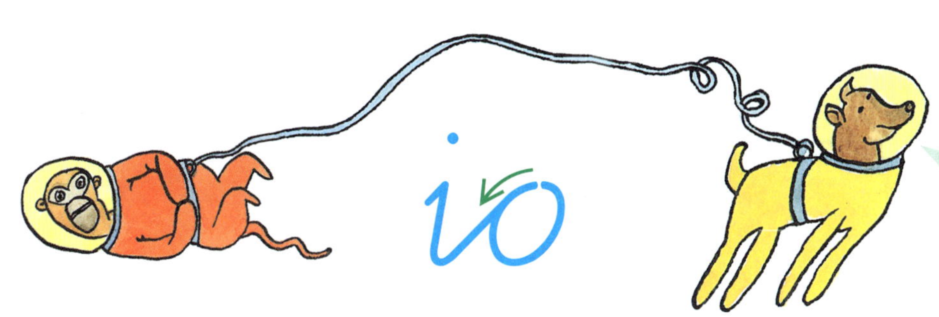

When o is the last letter in a word, it finishes at the top.

Write under each.

disco echo auto radio duo

trio dingo memo ghecko rhino

Pluto Apollo Galileo Soho Giotto

Theme sentences:

Debris may orbit Earth for a century!

In 1996, the satellite Cerise collided

with space junk, tumbling off-course.

What letters or joins do you need to practise?

Circle your best word.

Date ..../........./.........

Replace "nice" as you rewrite these sentences. Your words may be longer.

Lucy and Ben caught a nice ferry

across to the zoo. They had a nice

map to follow. First they saw nice

camels. Next were the nice giraffes.

Lucy had her photo taken in front of

the nice flamingoes. Ben liked the

nice seal show, and the nice dolphins,

too. The nice bears were sleepy, but not

How many points for your handwriting today?

Date ..../........../..........

Replace "nice" as you rewrite these sentences. Your words may be longer.

the nice lion, who was pacing up and

down. In the Australian section they

saw nice koalas, nice kangaroos, nice

emus, a nice platypus and two nice

wombats. In the bird aviary there were

lots of nice birds to admire, among

them a nice cockatoo. When it was time

to go, Lucy said, "What a nice day!"

Circle your best word.

Date .... / .... / ....

Finish each o in the centre at the top.
Don't lift your pencil.

Write under each.

oooo oooo oooo oooo oooo oooo

noodles smooth rooster cartoon

booster – rocket shampoo cookbook

Theme sentence:

The Moon is littered with old space probes, buggies with flat batteries, old experiments and landing gear.

What letters or joins do you need to practise?

1 2 3 4 5 How many points for your handwriting today?

Date .... / .... / ....

Use the crossbar of f to join. Curve up. No lifting.

Write under each.

flat flower fly float flea

flag flour flame flash flip

flood flock flies flare fluids

Theme sentence:

Nearly everything we know about planets and moons was discovered by space probes, explorers of the universe.

What letters or joins do you need to practise?

Circle your best word.

Date ..../........../..........

Keep the loop slim on each f.

Write under each.

aff eff iff off uff aff eff iff

effort raffle puffer office scruffy

blast-off lift-off different sniffles

Theme sentence:

Space probes have flown past, orbited, crashed into, landed or driven on most planets in our Solar System.

What letters or joins do you need to practise?

How many points for your handwriting today?

Date .... / .... / ....

Each rocket, shuttle, satellite and space probe is named, often with an inspirational message. Can you think of a good name?

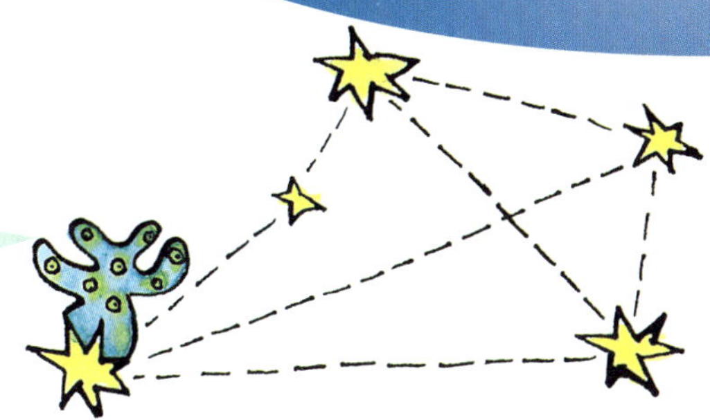

Write under each.

Explorer Surveyor Voyager Pioneer

Prospector Opportunity Pathfinder

Messenger Spirit ______________________

Theme sentence:

Space probes spend years travelling to photograph craters on Mercury, gases around Venus and canyons on Mars.

What letters or joins do you need to practise?

Circle your best word.

Date ..../........../..........

rr or rr

Dip after each r to finish it before joining. Lift if too hard.

Try joining double r, then lifting for each r.

arr arr err err irr irr orr orr

urr urr carry mulberry horrible

terrific sorry hurry error marry

Theme sentence:

Space probes sent to explore outer planets have nuclear power, as there is too little sunlight for solar panels.

What letters or joins do you need to practise?

1 2 3 4 5 How many points for your handwriting today?

Date ..../........../..........

nn

Stretch the join between double n for legibility. Each n has one wedge.

Write under each.

ann enn inn onn unn cannot

innings dinner tonnes announce

manned antenna anniversary

Theme sentence:

NASA's Deep Space Network tracks, commands and receives probe data using three 70-metre dish antennae.

What letters or joins do you need to practise?

Circle your best word.

Date ..../........./.........

mm

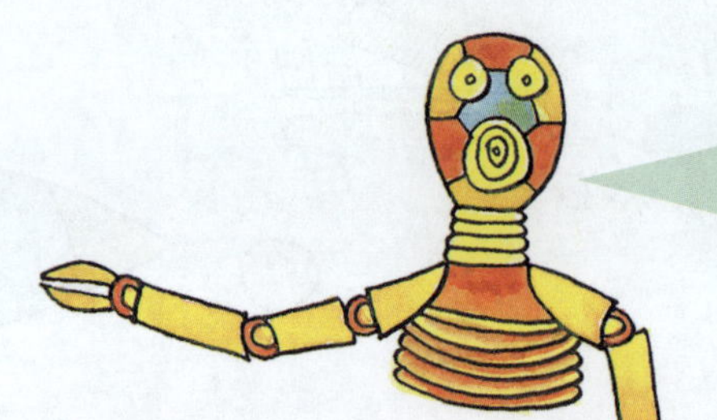

Each m has two wedges. Stretch the join between double m for legibility.

Write under each.

amm emm imm omm umm

mammal immense symmetry

gamma-ray command summit

Theme sentence:

As the Earth turns, an antenna in Canberra, California or Madrid is always in contact with each probe.

What letters or joins do you need to practise?

1 2 3 4 5

How many points for your handwriting today?

Date ..../........../..........

Stretch out between letters for legible writing.

Write under each.

eeee eeee eeee eeee eeee eeee eeee

need keep week street beef

sheet freeze beetle career speech

Theme sentences:

2004 — Spirit and Opportunity land on opposite sides of Mars. Each rover stands 1.5 metres and weighs 186 kg.

What letters or joins do you need to practise?

Circle your best word.

Date ..../........../..........

Give x a high exit, cross it, then the next letter can be dropped on.

Write under each.

axis oxygen galaxy exhale reflexes

hexagon extra sixth excited express

Explorer exercise mixture galaxy

Theme sentences:

Billions of pieces of space rock enter

our atmosphere every day. Most burn

up as a meteor or shooting star.

What letters or joins do you need to practise?

    How many points for your handwriting today?

Date .... / .... / ....

Curve up to the top of each l, then down with a covering stroke. Don't lift your pencil.

Write under each.

all ell ill oll ull allow yellow

vanilla lollipop trolley swollen

Challenger Apollo propelled satellite

Theme sentences:

Comets are chunks of dust, rock and ice from outer space. As they near the sun, they form tails of evaporation.

What letters or joins do you need to practise?

Circle your best word.

Date ..../........../..........

Double t can be crossed with one long line.

Write under each.

att ett itt ott utt cotton written

better matter forgotten attempt

battery shuttle jettison transmitter

Theme sentences:

Hale – Bopp comet, 1997, had two tails. Blue

gas tails can be hundreds of km long.

Yellow dust tails can be ten million km.

What letters or joins do you need to practise?

How many points for your handwriting today?

Date ..../........../..........

ess

Write under each.

ass ess iss uss address message

chess lioness tissue lesson grass

Messenger Cassini mission airless

Theme sentence:

2004 — The Stardust probe flew through dust and gas from the comet Wild 2, collecting samples and close-up photos.

What letters or joins do you need to practise?

Circle your best word.

Date .... / .... / ....

Write under each.

oss oss oss oss possible criss-cross

fossil fairy-floss possum tossing

Odyssey Ulysses crossbar glossary

Theme sentences:

In 2011, space probe Messenger started

to orbit the planet Mercury. In 2014,

Rosetta will place a lander on a comet.

What letters or joins do you need to practise?

How many points for your handwriting today?

Date .... / .... / ....

Each rocket, shuttle, satellite and space probe is named, often with an inspirational message. Can you think of a good name?

Write under each.

Friendship Gemini Echo Telstar Apollo

Luna-Orbiter Quick-Scat Early-Bird

Discovery Nimbus Destiny Stardust

Theme sentence:

Space tourists will fly into space for views of the Earth's oceans, clouds and continents — for a small fortune.

What letters or joins do you need to practise?

Circle your best word.

Date ..../........../..........

Plan a space voyage to anywhere in the universe.

If I blew a bubble in space, would it pop?

Name Your Spacecraft:

Your Destination:

Your Experiment:

Top-Secret Cargo:

Theme sentences:

Soon humans may set up a Moon base. Then, on to Mars — a six-month flight to a cold, dry, rocky, red planet.

What letters or joins do you need to practise?

1 2 3 4 5

How many points for your handwriting today?

Date .... / .... / ....

TEACHER'S NOTES

Short, daily handwriting lessons are far better than longer, infrequent lessons. Teacher modelling of lesson material on the blackboard to demonstrate the flow of handwriting is essential. The large join example on most pages can be traced. Don't copy directional or dropping-on arrows. All capitals remain printed and separate.

Page

1 Title page and list of contents

2 Introduction

3 Learning Features of Book 4

4–5 As a class, write each letter, then work out which carriage it belongs in (see reference card on inside back cover).

6–15 It is useful to liken the angle of diagonal joins to that of a slippery-slide to assist correct spacing between letters.

6–9 Two types of entries enhance legibility. Ensure the rounded entries aren't becoming pointed. With "x", the entry, right-to-left stroke and the exit are parallel. It must be crossed immediately, rather than coming back to cross it.

10 Answers will vary. Possible answers include: 1. mission, trip; 2. live, adapt; 3. made, built; 4. have; 5. spiders; 6. the, space; 7. affect, influence, change.

13 The crossbar of "f" is flexible. It is lower when joining to "e" and higher when joining to a top finisher.

15 It is useful to liken the angle of diagonal joins to that of a slippery-slide to assist correct spacing between letters.

16–17 Wedges are approximately two-thirds of the body height.

18 Uncoordinated writers or poor readers of cursive may find "r" difficult to write and prefer not to join from it. Ensure "r" finishes wholly with its downstroke whether it joins or not.

20 The small gap in the large example "o" is to highlight its correct rotation. Do not copy.

22 Sweep up joins have some retracing back down part of the ascenders/tall letters. These are called covering strokes. No lifting.

23–25 "Pencil lift" describes a deliberate stopping within a cursive word and restarting at the beginning of the next letter, to continue that word. It promotes fluency, speed and legibility by avoiding slow, messy looping.

Clockwise finishers are letters that finish on the left-hand-side of their form and do not lend themselves to joining. Simply go to the start of the next letter and continue writing.

27–28 Letters with "shoulders" or flat tops along the top blue line are dropped on to avoid a retracing or rocking motion over and back at the top of them. Dropping on is best after a diagonal join to these letters. All drop on letters are based on the "a" shape. An arrow is used to indicate where the exit stops and dropping on is required, throughout the *Write for Queensland* series. Do not copy the arrows.

29, 30, 32 Horizontal joins occur after letters that finish on or near the top blue line: top finishers "o", "r", "v" and "w". The join goes straight across, or dips slightly in the case of "r", to the next letter. The small gap in the large example "o" is to highlight its correct rotation.

32–33 The dip/flicking after "r" lends itself to dropping on the next shoulder letter, that is, "a", "c", "d", "g" or "q". This is optional and reminder arrows are on this page only.

34 Top finishers don't join to "e", as this does not allow for the correct position of the loop on letter "e".

35 Ensure "r" finishes wholly with its downstroke before sweeping up to the ascender.

37 Modified "f"—a diagonal join to "f" results in a loop.

38 When not joining from another letter, "f without a join" is used; that is, at the beginning of a word, after a capital or after a clockwise finisher.

40–44 Modified "s"—after a diagonal join, the flat shoulder of "s" disappears, leaving a point. Modified "s" should look pointed rather than rounded. Printed "s" may also be called "s without a join".

48 The small gap in each "o" on the large example is to highlight their correct rotation only. Do not copy.

51, 61 All capitals start at the top of their form and do not join. All capitals remain printed and separate.

56 Two types of entries enhance legibility. Ensure the rounded entries aren't becoming pointed. With "x", the entry, right-to-left stroke and the exit are parallel. It must be crossed immediately, rather than coming back to cross it.

59, 60 In order to keep double "s" looking right, the first type of "s" determines the second.

63 Teacher's Notes

64 Pen Skill Award

Inside back cover Reference Card—May be detached and contacted to the student's desk.

Pen Skill Award
has worked hard on handwriting
Assess your own handwriting.
Rounded Entries: Very Good Good Need Practice
Pointed Entries: Very Good Good Need Practice
Diagonal Joins: Very Good Good Need Practice
Horizontal Joins: Very Good Good Need Practice
Dropping On: Very Good Good Need Practice
Teacher's Comments:
Date:
Signed: